DINO

COLORING BOOK

BELONGE TO

Fun Dino Facts For Kids

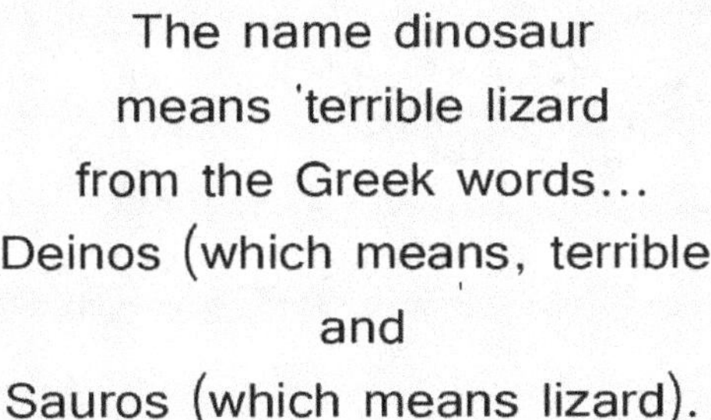

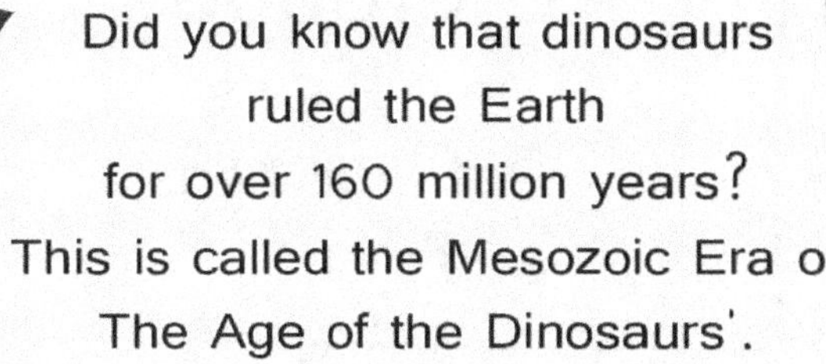

The name dinosaur
means 'terrible lizard
from the Greek words...
Deinos (which means, terrible)
and
Sauros (which means lizard).

Did you know that dinosaurs
ruled the Earth
for over 160 million years?
This is called the Mesozoic Era or
The Age of the Dinosaurs'.

The longest dinosaur was
the Seismosaurus.
(Greek for 'earth-shaking lizard')
measuring somewhere
around 40 meters.
and as long as five
double-decker buses!

So far 100 species
of dinosaurs have
been discovered in Britain!

Most dinosaurs were actually
vegetarians - not meat eaters!
They're not that scary after all...

The dinosaur
with the longest name is...
Micropachycephalosaurus!

Coelophysis were the fasten
dinosaurs around.
Short distance sprints of those
dinosaurs reached up to 30 miles..

Over 700 different species
of dinosaurs have been found...
but many believe there are many
more new and dinosaur
species still to be discovered!

The dinosaurs may have
ended up being huge,
but they all came from eggs.

Different Types of Dinosaurs

Theropods
- Meat Eaters
- Powerful Legs
- Short Arms

Sauropods
- Long necks
- Long tails
- Walked on four feet

Stegosaurs
- Slow
- Bony plates or spikes

Ceratopsians
- 4 legged body
- 3 horns
- bony frill

Ornithopods
- Walkes and ran on two back feet

Ankylosauria
- Bony armour

Dd IS FOR
DINOSAUR

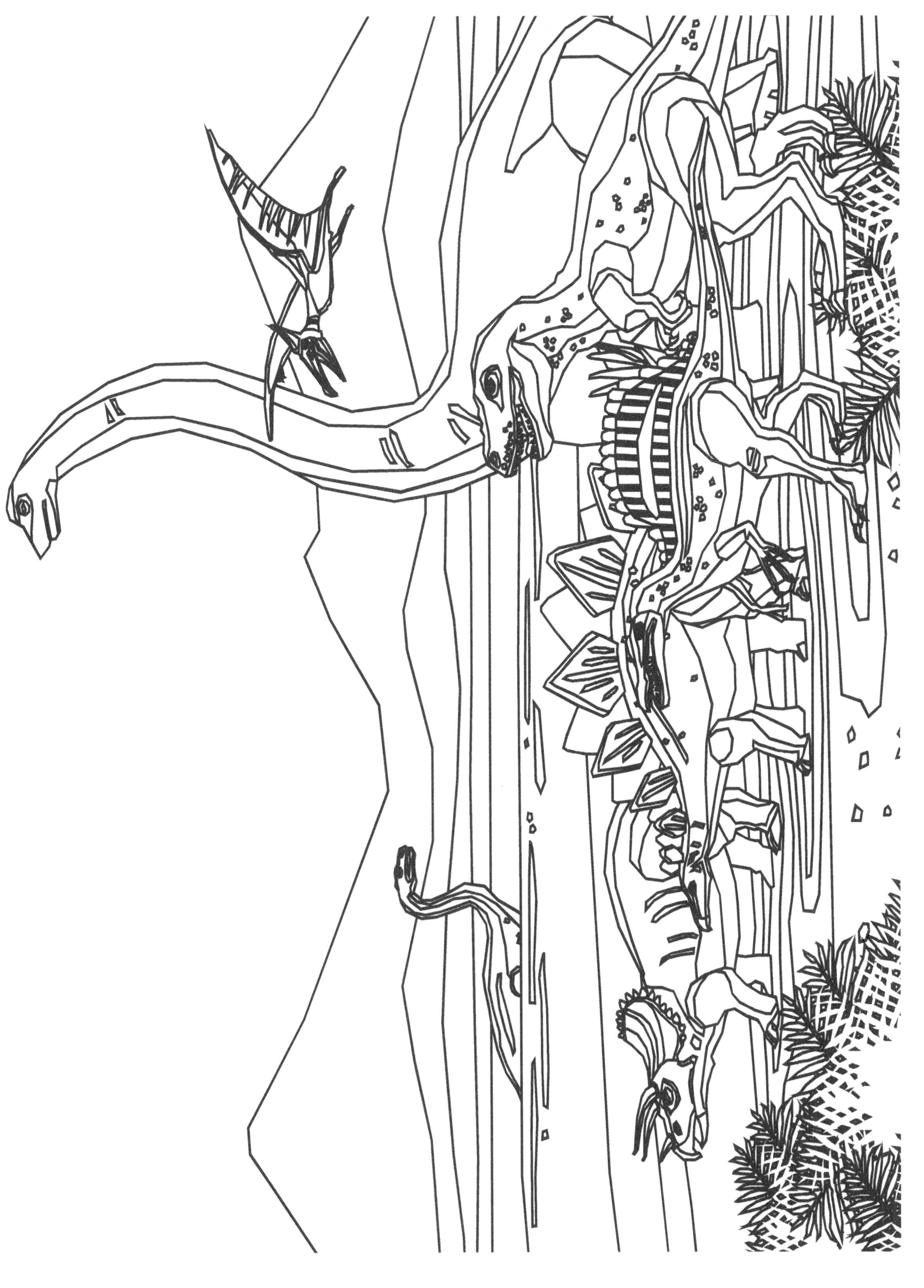

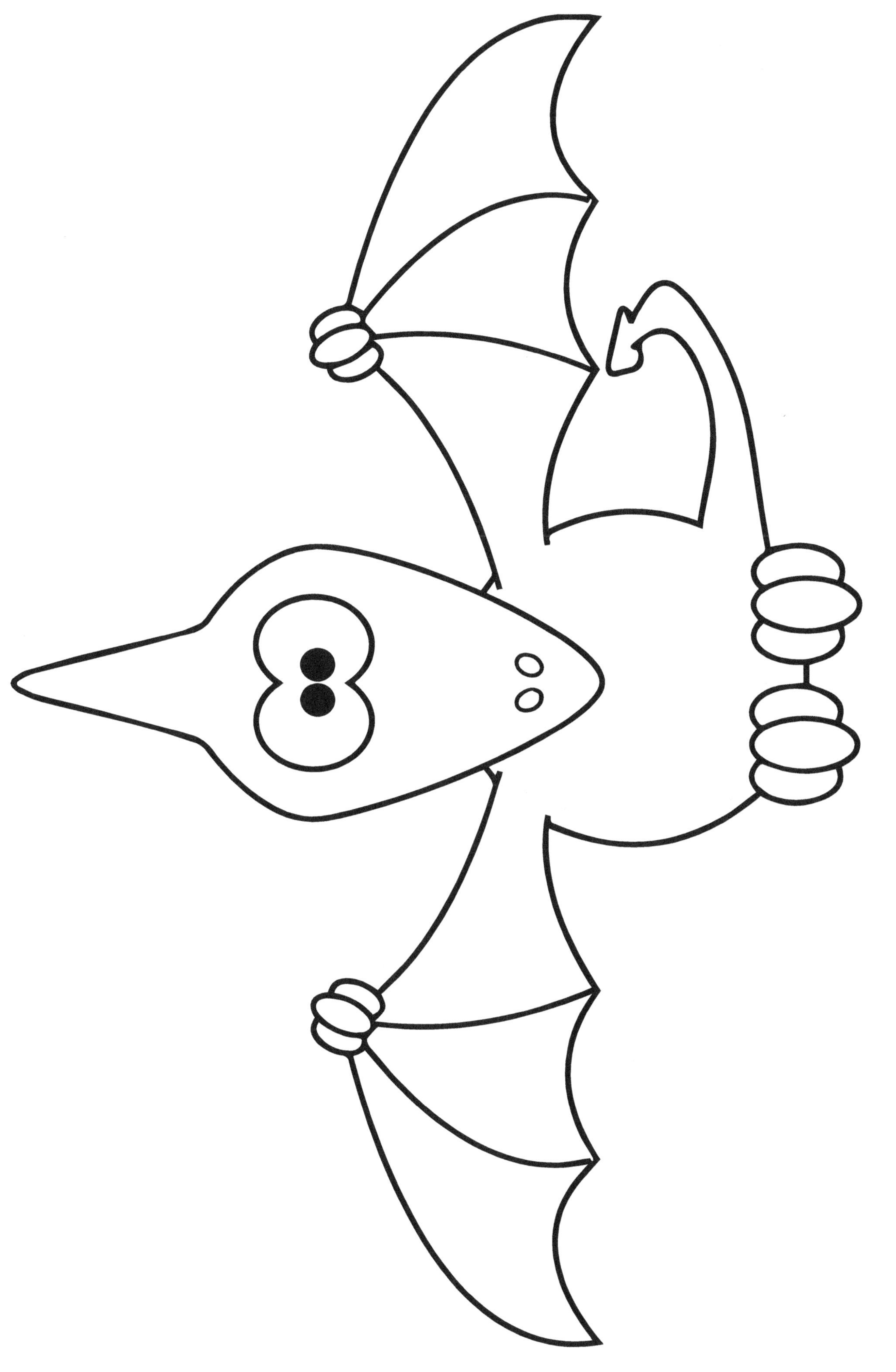

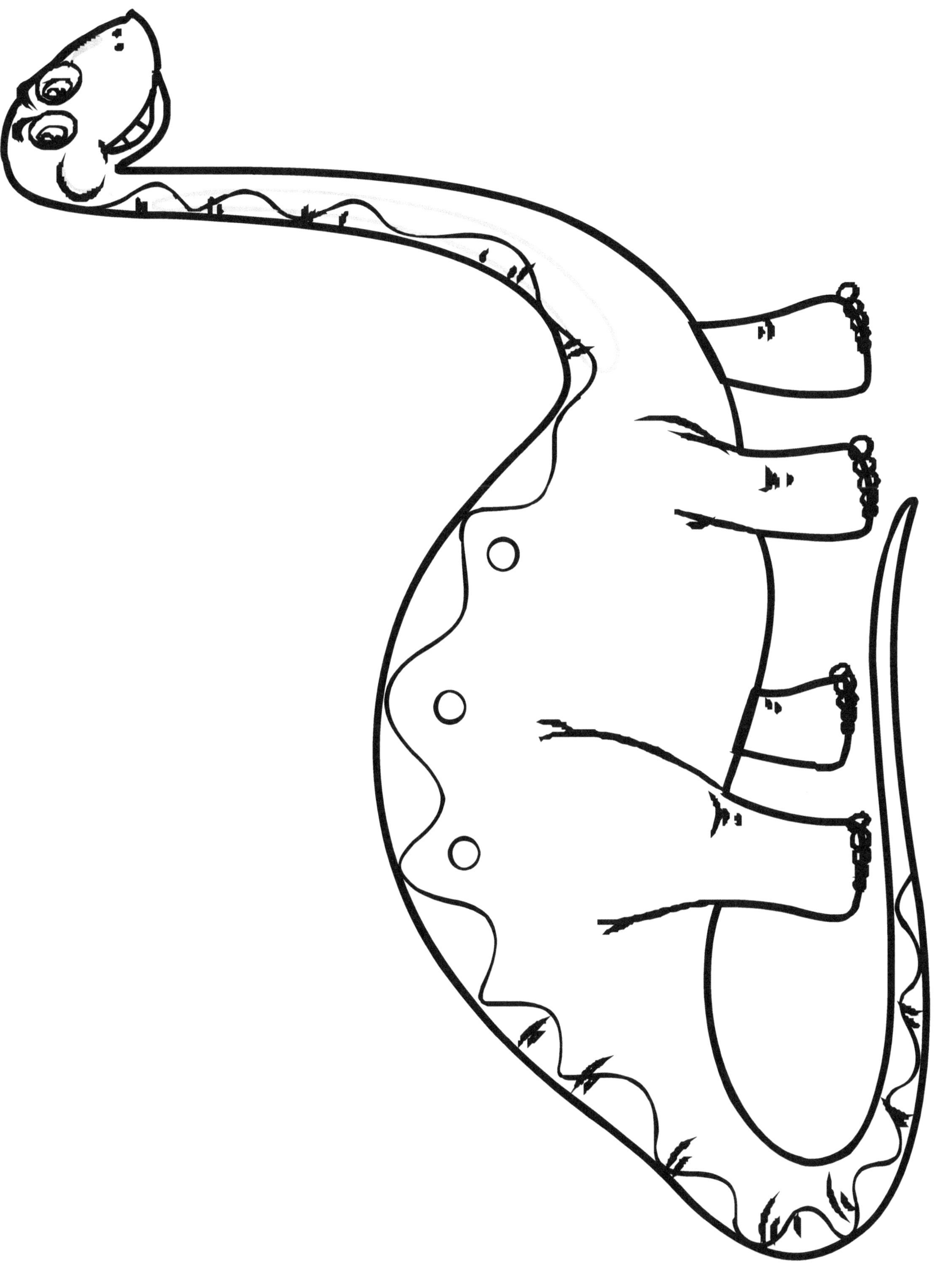

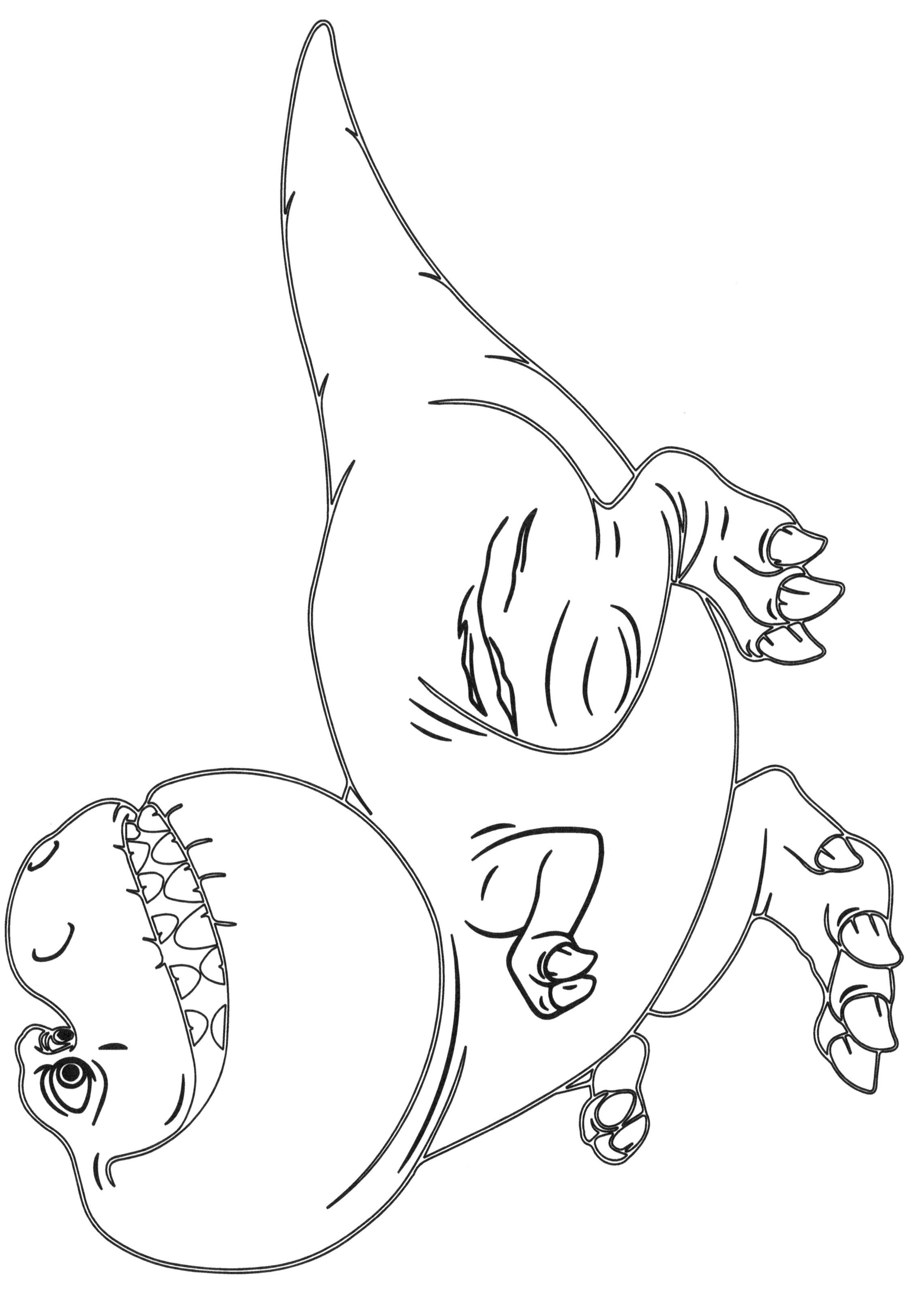

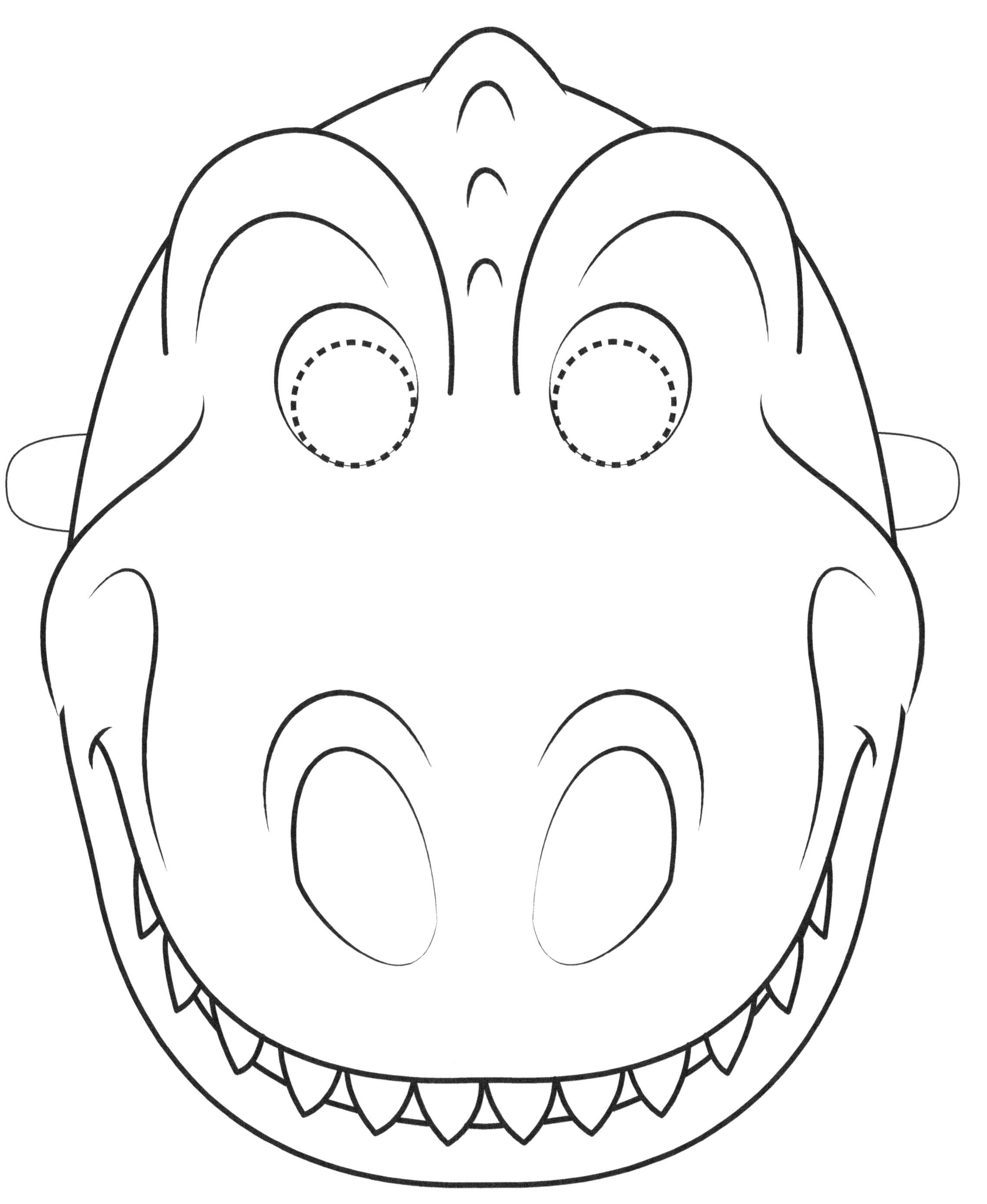

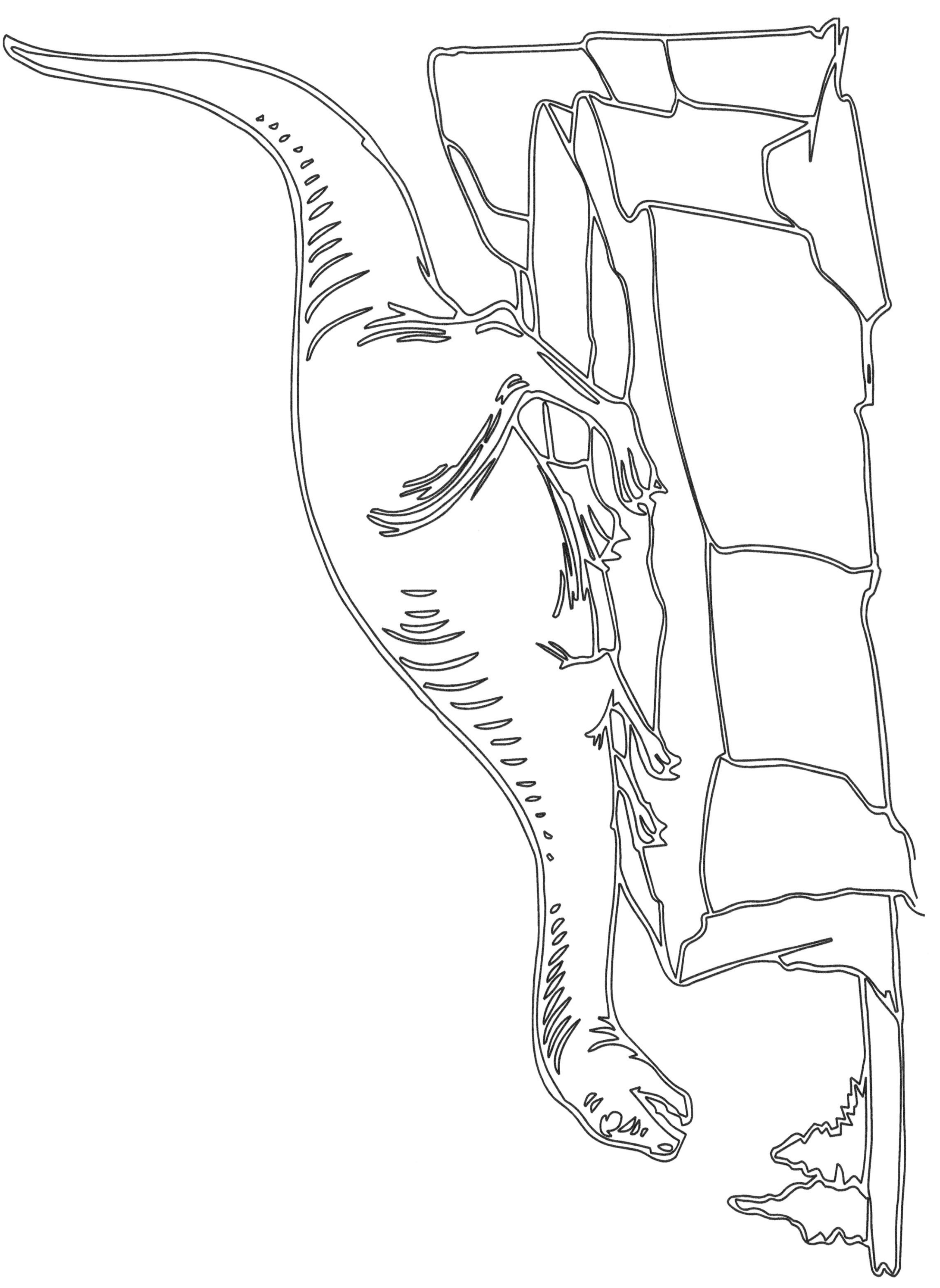

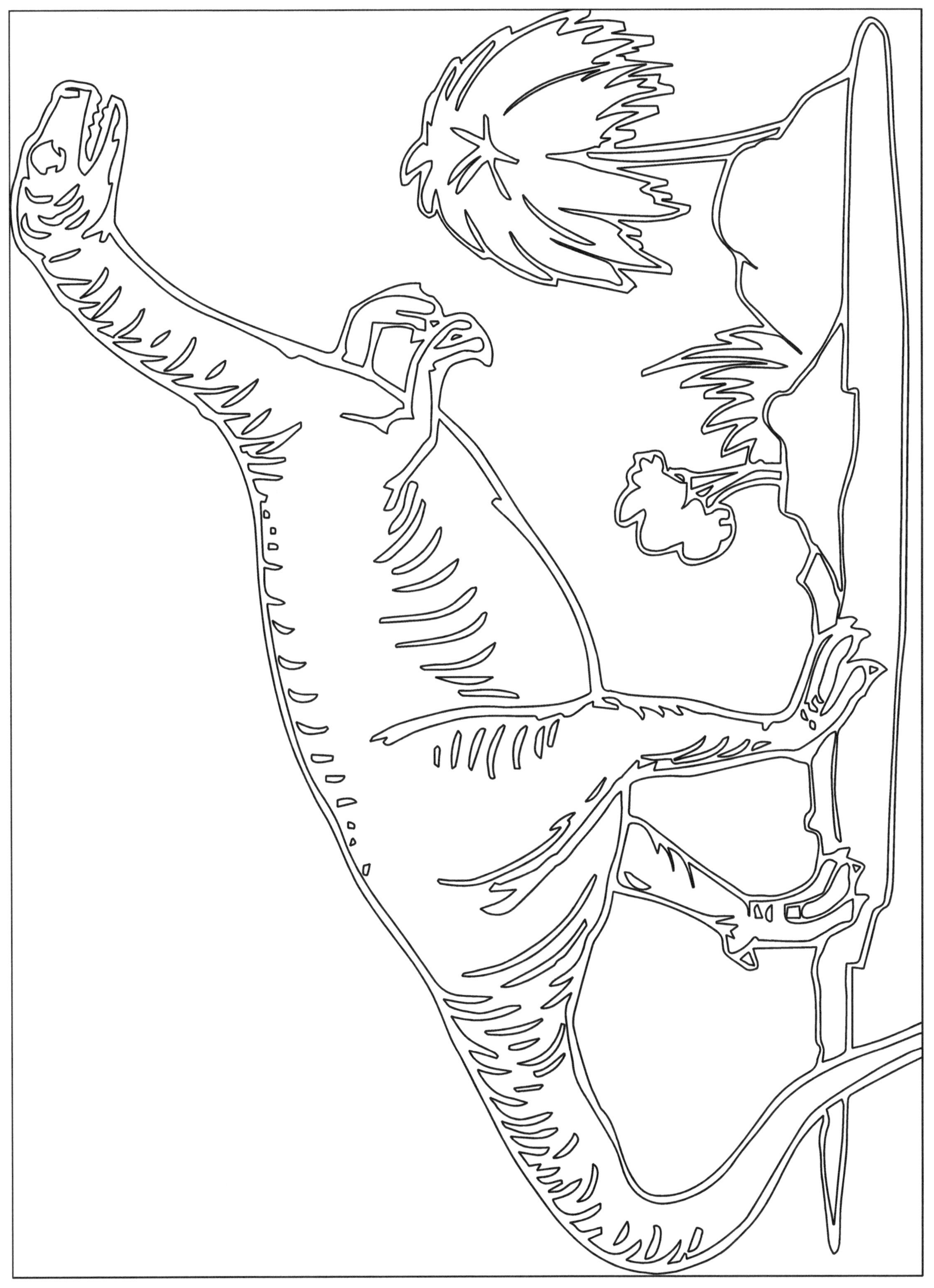

COLOR TEST PAGE

COLOR TEST PAGE